First published 1980
This edition published 1982
Reprinted 1984

ISBN 0 7134 3370 1

Printed by R J Acford, Chichester, Sussex
for the Publishers Batsford Academic and
Educational
4 Fitzhardinge Street, London W1H 0AH

For George, with love

Frontispiece: **A mudlark, from "London Labour
and London Poor" by Henry Mayhew**

Acknowledgment

The Author and Publishers would like to thank the
following for their kind permission to reproduce
copyright illustrations in this book: Bedfordshire
County Record Office for fig 53; the Trustees of the
British Museum for figs 44, 45; BBC Hulton Picture
Library for figs 1, 2, 3, 4, 5, 8, 12, 13, 14, 16, 18,
19, 20, 21, 22, 25, 26, 27, 29, 32, 34, 36, 39, 40,
41, 46, 47, 48, 49, 55, 57; Mary Evans Picture
Library for figs 15, 43, 52, 54, 58; National Portrait
Gallery for figs 7, 24, 59, 60; Newton Chambers &
Co Ltd for fig 33; Norfolk Museums Service,
Norwich Castle Museum for fig 6; Royal Com-
mission on Ancient Monuments, Scotland for fig 37
(Crown Copyright); the Science Museum, London
for figs 31, 35, 62 (Crown Copyright); the Tate
Gallery, London for figs 23, 28; the Victoria and
Albert Museum for figs 9, 10 (Crown Copyright).
Appreciation also to Pat Hodgson for the picture
research on this book.

Contents

The Illustrations

1 The Changing Face of England

The Industrial Revolution is the term used to describe the period of British history during which Britain changed from an agricultural to an industrial economy. There are really no precise starting and finishing dates for this period as there are, for example, for the reign of a king. In this book the dates 1760 and 1833 are taken to mark the beginning and end of the time of immense industrial change. Historians may argue a little over precisely dating the period, but no-one can argue with this fact: in 1750 England had an agricultural economy and the vast majority of the population lived in the countryside; but by 1850 most of the population lived in towns and earned their living from the great new industries on which the country's economy was by then based.

1   The changing face of England. Into the country landscape come imposing features of the Industrial Revolution, the bridges and the steam train.

What caused the change?

Men did not suddenly become inventive half-way through the eighteenth century. Indeed, many of the machines which played an important part in the Industrial Revolution had first been made many years earlier. But they had not been widely adopted and their potential had not been recognized.

As the population grew, so too did the demand for manufactured goods. It was this increased demand which prompted enterprising businessmen to see how the manufacturing process could be developed. It is as if from the 1760s all existing technical knowledge and separate inventions came together like the pieces of a great jigsaw

2   Matthew Boulton.

6

puzzle. And one of the most important factors causing all the pieces to fit together was power.

At first the new machines were run on water power, but then came steam. James Watt's steam engine was produced at Matthew Boulton's engineering works at Soho, Birmingham. When the diarist James

3   The introduction of steam power, one of the most important factors of the Industrial Revolution, caught the imagination of the cartoonists of the time. This cartoon of 1807 predicted that people would be (from left to right) walking by steam, riding by steam and flying by steam.

Boswell visited these works in 1776, Boulton proudly declared:

> I sell here, sir, what all the world desires to have — power.

This was no idle boast. The invention and manufacture of steam-powered machinery meant that man at last became independent of the uncertainties of wind and water power to drive his machines.

Effects of the change

This book is about the effect which the changing work patterns had on people's lives. First of all, the regularity of work and manufacture made possible by the new machines and factories was a great change for people who were used to agricultural work regulated by the seasons.

The mill-owners and their foremen found that children, who had not got into the habit of working as they pleased, made better employees than their parents who never before had had to work regular hours, day in day out, week in week out. Therefore children were employed whenever possible and, looking back, their lives were an almost unceasing round of exhausting work in appalling conditions.

Today we regard some of the work done by children in the Industrial Revolution as unbelievably cruel. For example, who in their right mind would now expect a six-year-old to spend all day alone in the dark of a mine tunnel hundreds of feet below ground? There was a great deal of exploitation of children in the mines and factories. It is human nature to try to obtain the maximum from the minimum and the industrialists realized that children were the most amenable employees for the routine work.

But we should remember that during the period of the Industrial Revolution childhood was not regarded as an important stage of growing up as it is today. Children of the well-to-do were expected to look and behave like adults as soon as possible, and certainly before they were in their teens. Children from poor homes were expected to make their contribution to the family income almost as soon as they could walk. This was a reflection of society's beliefs at the time, not deliberate cruelty.

Another thing to remember is that people who did not live in the industrial areas could not have known what went on in the factories and mines. People travelled very little, because travelling was uncomfortable, slow and expensive. News and information therefore spread very slowly.

However, when people did become aware of the dreadful treatment of children in industry, reforms were demanded. The Factory Act of 1833 was the first effective legislation against exploitation of children in British industry. It was to be followed by the great programme of social reforms for which the Victorian age (1837-1901) is famous.

2 The Structure of Society

In every country at this period society was divided into quite rigid classes. In Britain at the beginning of the Industrial Revolution period the two main classes were the landowners and those who worked for them. By the end of the period many of these farm labourers had gone to live in towns and cities. The middle class, so large today, was very small, especially outside the towns.

The landowners

Within the landowning class there was much variation of rank. There were the great aristocratic families, like the Northumberlands and Bedfords, who had enormous estates scattered round the country. But there were many more small farmers, called yeomen farmers, who owned their land and farmed it themselves, with the help of their families and a few hired labourers. These yeomen farmers guarded their independence jealously. Thomas Rowlandson, the great caricaturist of English society at the time, drew a yeoman farmer character whom he called John Bull. The caricature immortalized this type of Englishman.

The middle class

In the market towns the number of shopkeepers and tradesmen was growing. As the towns expanded, these people became more important and wealthy. They and the increasing number of professional men, such as lawyers and doctors, formed the basis of the middle class which was to grow so rapidly during Queen Victoria's reign (1837-1901).

Farm labourers

Most of the rest of the population at the beginning of the Industrial Revolution worked for the landowners. There was much variation in this class too. At one extreme were those who worked for the great landowners. They were tenants of farms far larger than those of many a "John Bull". At the other extreme were the itinerant labourers who were hired for one year at a time at the great autumn hiring fairs. In between was the bulk of the population, the agricultural labourers.

4   John Bull.

5   A farm labourer, drawn in the 1790s.

Even these people at this time had a degree of economic independence. Most had gardens around their cottages where they grew whatever they liked and kept a few hens. On the common land around the village they might also keep a cow or a pig. This all helped to stretch the family's meagre wages, and also gave some protection against price rises. But this economic independence was lost in the country's shift from an agricultural to an industrial economy. By the end of the period those farm labourers who had gone to live in the towns no longer had gardens where they could grow their own food. And even the people who remained in the country had lost their right to graze animals on the newly enclosed common land.

Future prospects

Compared with today, society was fairly static during this period. Even though there was a trend towards the towns, people moved only slowly and to nearby towns. Communications were so bad and travelling so difficult that only the really desperate travelled far. Most people lived and died in the same district in which they had been born. There was also relatively little movement from one social class to the other. Of course, within the classes, there was movement as the fortunes of individual families rose and fell. But the general opinion was that if a man was born into a particular position in society, then that was his place and there he should stay.

This rule could be broken, of course, if you had money. In this respect British society was far more flexible than, for example, the French. If a man from a poor background was successful and became rich, he was usually accepted by the gentry. His children certainly were, and might even achieve the ranks of the lesser nobility. Many men at this time showed that it was possible to rise out of one's class. Josiah Wedgwood (1730-95) was the son of a craftsman potter. Josiah experimented with new techniques of manufacture and when he died was worth £500,000 (an incredible sum) and had fulfilled his ambition to be "Vase Maker General to the Universe" — a boast which is almost as true today as then, with Wedgwood china being exported all over the world. Robert Owen is another example. He came from a humble Welsh home, but by the age of nineteen was superintendant (a type of manager) of a Manchester cotton mill. He persuaded the owners to buy New Lanark

6   An aristocratic family in the 1780s. Sir Robert and Lady Buxton and their daughter Anne. (Painting by Henry Walton.)

where he put his humane ideas into practice and which he eventually owned.

The great aristocratic families were also less rigid in their view of their own importance than some of their continental counterparts. Much of London's Bloomsbury was a speculative building development by the Bedford family. Few self-respecting continental aristocrats, ever on the defence of the family's dignity, would have stooped to such a commercial venture — even if the alternative was bankruptcy. Again, in contrast to their continental peers, the English aristocracy were often in the forefront of recognizing and using the new inventions and improvements. The Duke of Bridgewater had one of the first canals in the country cut across his land to take coal from his mine at Worsley to the growing town of Manchester.

The majority of children, however, knew exactly what their futures would be: a repeat version of the life led by their parents, their grandparents and probably (since life expectancy then was so much shorter than it is today) their great-grandparents.

The eldest son of an aristocratic family would automatically inherit the family's whole estate. He might not want to, but the system of primogeniture was so well established that probably few fathers or sons ever questioned it. It ensured that estates were not broken up and remained in large and therefore economic units. On the continent, especially in France, on the other hand, the custom was to divide the land equally between all the sons in a family. This gradually reduced the size of farms and the prosperity of the families running them.

The younger sons of landowners at least had a choice: to go into the Church or the army. At this time, of course, the Church meant the Church of England. Roman Catholics were still regarded with suspicion, if no longer with hostility. There was at least one church on most of the large estates. The clergyman was often chosen by the owner of the estate, and so, not surprisingly, many a clergyman was the younger brother of the local landowner. The clergyman had a pleasant job. The appointment was generally for life and, in return for a good house and very adequate income, he could do as much or as little church work as his conscience permitted. Indeed, it was at this period that

the staid, rather lazy establishment of the Church of England was shaken by the reforming zeal of John Wesley (1703-91) and the Methodist movement.

The army enrolled younger sons of the aristocracy and gentry as officers. Those who wanted to spend their time hunting, drinking and gambling could and did. In peace time it was difficult for those who were more ambitious to get on. But for much of the Industrial Revolution England was at war with France and this gave an opportunity to soldiers with ability to prove their worth and gain advancement.

Sons of tradesmen and small farmers would help in the family business or be apprenticed to learn a trade from a master craftsman. Boys from these homes who joined the army or navy were unlikely to start with the advantage of an officer's commission. However, the long years of war against Napoleon forced the British army and navy into a greater professionalism, so that experience and ability were more frequently rewarded than ever before. Even so, John Shipp was exceptional. He was a boy from the poorest and most despised of all backgrounds — the workhouse — who joined up when he was twelve, rose to become a commissioned officer, sold his commission to pay off gambling debts,

rejoined as a private soldier and again rose to the rank of commissioned officer.

Girls had even less choice about their future than their brothers. Girls from wealthy homes would very often have to marry a husband chosen by their parents. The choice was based more on land and wealth than on the compatibility of the couple. Having become wives, the girls would organize the domestic side of their husband's estates, just as their mothers had done.

In poor families girls, like their brothers, helped their parents almost as soon as they could do anything useful. By their early teens they would work alongside their mother, at home or in the fields. They probably had more freedom in choosing a husband than girls from rich families, but after marriage, despite many pregnancies, they went on working to supplement the family's income. Too often this was reflected in bad health and was one reason for the high mortality rate among babies.

8   A clergyman with some of his congregation.

7   A country squire on the left is visited by his sporting neighbour and his servant.

3 Homes and Health

The contrast between social classes described in Chapter 2 was reflected in every aspect of life, and especially in the homes in which children grew up.

The many fine Georgian buildings which survive today were the homes of the well-to-do. Throughout the period, as the country became more and more prosperous, the standard of wealthy homes rose. John Nash and the brothers Robert and John Adam, drawing inspiration from the remains of Classical and Roman buildings, became sought-after architects for the wealthy and fashionable.

Even so, the fine terraces and spacious rooms of the houses built by the rich were seldom matched by good plumbing or sanitation. Baths were taken in round or oval tubs. The servants often had to carry the heavy jugs of hot water up several flights of stairs to fill the bath tubs. When Buckingham House, later Buckingham Palace, was first built it had no bathrooms at all.

In 1775 Alexander Cummings, a watchmaker by trade, patented a U-bend water closet. After it had been flushed, some water remained in the bend, and this prevented the blow-back of poisonous sewer gas which had been a hazard with earlier designs. Later,

9   A rich home. The villa at Kenwood designed by Robert Adam.

Joseph Bramah made improvements to Cummings' patent. In principle, his design is what we use today. Of course, during the Industrial Revolution such water closets were only found in the homes of the wealthy, and even there the drains were largely inadequate. More enlightened and practical home-owners built cess-pits, but these were emptied infrequently and often overflowed and so did little to improve the general problem.

Housing for the poor, unlike wealthy housing, did not improve. In 1815 R.W. Dickinson recorded that "the houses of poor farming peasants in Lancashire are mostly made of wattle and daub". Wattle and daub means interwoven tree branches plastered with a mixture of clay and mud. Dwellings had been built in this way in medieval times, at least four hundred years earlier! In 1825 the *Quarterly Review* claimed that few cottages were now "without a brick or stone or wood floor, without stairs to the chambers, without plastering on the walls and without doors and windows tolerably watertight". The fact that the *Review* considered this to be proof of a great improvement in housing shows how bleak and uncomfortable the homes of most country children in the Industrial Revolution must have been.

But the homes of children who lived in the newly developing industrial towns were even worse. At least in the country people breathed fresh air, there was little noise, and although conditions inside the cottages were usually very cramped, there was plenty of space outside. The new towns were very different.

10   A country home in 1793.

Homes in industrial towns

The industrial towns grew haphazardly as people drifted to them from the surrounding countryside, attracted by the chance of a job at one of the new factories. There was nowhere for them to live, and so many of the mill- and factory-owners, being rich men and needing workers, built houses for their employees. They knew that the people who would live in them were coming from poor homes, and so they wasted no money on good building materials, drains, or water-supplies. Gardens were quite out of the

11 A street of houses in Lancashire built in the Industrial Revolution.

question. Instead, rows and rows of mean little "back-to-back" houses were built. They got this name because the back walls of the houses in one street were the back walls of the houses in the street parallel with it. Most back-to-back houses had two rooms upstairs and two rooms down and the rooms at the back were very dark because, of course, they had no windows.

There was no lavatory, just a "privy" at

the end of the street shared by several families. It was not private and the inadequate drain was usually blocked and overflowing. The water-supply was a tap, often just by the privy, shared by all the families in the street. The supply was erratic. Sometimes it was turned on for only an hour or two each day, and in dry weather it often failed completely. Then the family, tired after a day's work, had to fetch and pay for water from the local water-carrier. In such circumstances washing anything, even face and hands, was an immense luxury.

As the Industrial Revolution progressed and towns became ever bigger, so the pressure on housing increased. For example, Liverpool's population was 5,000 in 1700, but 77,000 by 1801. Every available space was occupied, from cellars to attics. According to a survey taken in Liverpool in 1848, there were 39,000 people living in 7,800 cellars. Even allowing for some exaggeration, this figure shows how shocking conditions were. An Italian visitor to London in the 1820s remarked that, of course the English could not throw their arms around and gesticulate like the Italians, because there simply was not enough room in their homes.

Furniture

The furniture used by the different social classes showed the same contrast as their housing. The very rich had furniture made by the great master cabinet-makers and designers. Thomas Chippendale (c.1718-79), George Hepplewhite (d. 1786) and Thomas Sheraton (1751-1806). The very poor had crude, roughly assembled benches and tables. Although only the very rich could afford furniture from the workshops of the three great cabinet-makers, these men still had a great influence on English furniture. They published books of their designs, so that any good craftsman could make a similar piece, perhaps using a local wood, rather than an exotic imported one.

Most of the population never saw furniture of this standard or style. Bad roads and poor communications meant that small towns and villages had to be almost entirely self-sufficient for everyday needs. Therefore, every place had a carpenter or two, and it was furniture made by local carpenters which graced most homes of the period. Good, bad or indifferent, it reflected the skill of the craftsman and the price his customer could pay.

12 A cellar home in London.

16

Windows

Homes during the Industrial Revolution were dark. Lighting was by candle or oil-lamp, although gas was beginning to reach richer homes by the end of the period. (In 1802 Matthew Boulton had his engineering works lit by gas, a pioneering step.) However, it was the lack of windows that really made homes dark. It also meant that houses were stuffy. Houses with fewer than six windows were taxed at eight shillings (40p), those with seven windows at £1 and those with eight windows at £1.13s. (£1.65). Therefore, to save money, householders often bricked up "unnecessary" windows. As often as not staircases had no windows on them and were dark and dangerous.

Cooking

In the early part of the period food was still cooked on open hearths. The risk of accidental fire was therefore ever-present. This is one reason why in most larger houses the kitchens were far from the main living rooms.

13 A kitchen scene, with meat roasting on a spit. Thomas Robinson's kitchen range was an improvement on this equipment.

Another reason is that it lessened the cooking smells which reached the living rooms.

Meat was roasted on spits hung over the fires. To ensure that the meat was cooked evenly, the spits had to be turned. This was usually done by means of a treadwheel. A small child or a dog had to walk round and round inside the treadwheel.

Thomas Robinson's invention of the kitchen range in 1780 was a great step forward. The fire was enclosed, and on one side was an oven, on the other a tank for heating water. Food could also be cooked on the top of the range.

Food

People living in the country had plenty of home-grown food, either from their cottage gardens or from the kitchen gardens of their estates. Many foreign visitors to England commented on how much most English agricultural workers ate. Meat for them was not such a luxury as it was for their European counterparts. Poultry, home-cured bacon and ham, and game poached from the surrounding woods varied the usual diet of bread, vegetables and cheese.

In towns, very rich families had supplies sent up from their estates. Prosperous merchants could afford to buy food from shops and markets. But the growing class of poor industrial workers were at a great disadvantage. They had no gardens in which to grow food or keep hens. Wages were so low that, to get enough money for the family to survive, the mother had to go out to work too. At the end of a ten- or twelve-hour day she had no energy left to shop or cook, even if she had the facilities for cooking, which was unlikely. As a result, the poor relied almost entirely on bought food, which was usually of poor quality and often adulterated.

18

Milk was watered down, butter and cheese were coloured artificially to disguise bad patches, and sudsy water from washing linen was added to weak beer to give it a good head of froth. It is not surprising that children, living on such food, suffered from diseases like tuberculosis and rickets, nor that typhoid and dysentery were common.

Public health

The connection between poor diet, bad housing, appalling sanitation and a high mortality rate was not really understood at the beginning of the Industrial Revolution — although even if it had been understood, things would probably not have been much different. The cheapest possible housing would still have been put up for the industrial poor. It was not until the first serious outbreak of cholera occurred in 1831 that attempts were made to improve the situation.

The work of Edwin Chadwick was particularly influential in improving conditions. He was one of the first to appreciate that poor housing and bad health are closely related, and he worked hard to get reforms. His *Report on the Sanitary Conditions of the Labouring Population*, published in 1842, showed how bad conditions were throughout the period of industrial development. He found, for example, that many workers in Manchester died at the age of 17; in Leeds they reached 19 years of age; but in Liverpool only 15. In marked contrast, rich people in Leeds could expect to live for about 44 years, and in Liverpool for 35 years.

Hospitals and medicine

Most of today's best-known London hospitals already existed by this period, and important towns like Bristol also had a hospital. And yet very little was understood about

14   The Rahere ward at St Bartholomew's Hospital, London, in 1832.

disease and medicine. Doctors had few medicines and only the most primitive instruments with which to operate. They wore their ordinary clothes while operating, and they did not bother to wash their hands or sterilize their instruments because the importance of hygiene and cleanliness was still not realized. Indeed, it is amazing that without anaesthetics or antiseptics any patient ever survived an operation. But patients did survive, and some surgeons achieved a high degree of skill. William Cheselden of St Thomas's Hospital could remove a stone from the bladder in less than a minute.

Nurses

Nursing and midwifery were not yet respectable professions for a girl. Consequently, the few nurses and midwives there were were untrained and irresponsible — rather like Mrs Sarah Gamp, the drink-sodden character created by Charles Dickens in his novel *Martin Chuzzlewit*. She was, of course, a caricature, but there was undoubtedly a good deal of truth in Dickens' description of her.

It is remarkable that so many children survived. Progress was gradually being made. The Hunter brothers, William (1718-63) and John (1728-93), did much to make surgery more precise and, therefore, safer. Because they needed a good supply of bodies, for their practical work in anatomy, they were often accused of employing body-snatchers to cut down corpses from the gallows. Whether that was true or not, it was largely due to the efforts of John Hunter that surgery became a science and a profession, to the benefit of future generations.

15   Charles Dickens' drink-sodden nurse character, Mrs Gamp, proposes a toast to her friend.

4 Education

Education was not rated very highly at this time. Most adults thought that the most useful thing a child could learn was how to help increase the family income. In this case they did not need schooling — they needed practical experience. The majority of children gained such experience either by helping in the family business or by going out to work in fields, mines or mills. Apprentices learnt a trade, but this could hardly be called "education" either. Education, of a kind, was available to all sections of society, but it was up to the individual to take advantage of it. And for most of the population economic necessity ensured that children had no education.

Education for the rich
The sons of the rich usually had tutors at home. Tutors were often the younger sons of families of the growing middle class. Otherwise, they might be curates who had

16   Rugby public school in the 1830s. The headmaster, assistant masters and ushers take their different classes in one schoolroom.

failed to get a parish appointment. Tutoring was generally a last resort as a means of earning one's living. Therefore, tutors were probably not very inspiring teachers. Also, in an age when a man was judged by his ability to shoot and ride well, rather than by his formal education, there was little encouragement for either tutor or pupil to take the lessons seriously.

Generally speaking, in rich families the most attention was paid to the education of the younger sons, for they would have to make their way in the world without the advantage of the income which their eldest brother would enjoy when he inherited the family's estate.

Public schools

After the Industrial Revolution, from the middle of Queen Victoria's reign (1837-1901), the number of public schools was to rise very rapidly, as the new industries brought wealth to a wider range of the population. But during the period covered by this book (1760-1833) there were only nine public schools of importance: Eton, Harrow, Winchester, Westminster, Charterhouse, Shrewsbury, Rugby, St Pauls and Merchant Taylors. Several of these had been founded specifically to teach poor boys. This idea was now abandoned as wealth and social status had become more important. When the 5th Duke of Hamilton went to Winchester at the age of thirteen, he was automatically put at the head of the school because there was no other pupil of such a high social rank. At Eton only peers' sons ever came top of the form.

But boys who were sent to public school did not have an easy time. Pupils have left accounts of inadequate food, dirty, gloomy, unheated buildings, and sadistic punishments for the most trivial offences. Many of the punishments were carried out by the other boys, the masters merely turning a blind eye. The fagging system was particularly hated. The junior boys were at the beck and call of the older ones who delighted in setting them impossible tasks so that their failure could be punished with a flogging. *Tom Brown's Schooldays* reflects the awful conditions and atrocious education of many of the public schools of this period.

Grammar schools

The sons of yeomen farmers and prosperous townsmen usually went for a year or two to the local grammar school, where life was less hard. The standard of these schools, too, had declined. In 1795 Lord Chief Justice Kenyon complained that grammar schools were "empty walls without scholars and everything neglected but the receipt of salaries". This was a generalization, but the ideals of the grammar schools founded in Edward VI's reign (1547-53), as many had been, were certainly no longer followed, and the subjects taught in them had not developed much since then. As in the public schools, the emphasis was on the Classics, mostly Latin but with Greek occasionally for a change. Science was taught if a member of the staff was interested in it, and particularly if the school was near an expanding industrial area where the effects of new scientific developments were obvious. In agricultural districts such developments were not obvious and "science" consisted of improving livestock and crops, both strictly a matter of practical application.

The quality of teaching in the schools varied according to the interest and ability of the headmaster and his few staff. The schools were independent. The concept of an education authority and a set standard of education for the whole country was many years into the future.

Universities

Most of the students at the universities of the day, Oxford, Cambridge, Edinburgh, Glasgow, St Andrews and Trinity College, Dublin, were the sons of aristocrats. In fact, the universities were little more than an extension of the public schools, with very little care or attention paid to either learning or discipline. The dons seemed no more interested in education than the school-masters. When Richard Watson was appointed Professor of Chemistry at Cambridge in 1764 he said he "had never read a syllable on the subject nor seen a single experiment, but I was tired of mathematics and natural philosophy and [wished] to try my strength in a new pursuit". In 1771 he was appointed Regius Professor of Divinity at the same university. He said that "on being raised to this distinguished office, I immediately applied myself with great eagerness to the study of Divinity".

Students from poorer backgrounds went to universities to learn, so that they could make a career for themselves, usually in the Church or in Law. But their efforts to learn must have been hampered by the general attitude of the dons and the rich students. Dr Newsome, head of Hertford College, Oxford, wrote to one of his students, Charles James Fox (1749-1806), the future Whig politician, who was visiting Paris with his father:

As to trigonometry, it is a matter of entire indifference to the other geometricians of the college . . . whether they proceed to the other branches of mathematics immediately, or wait a term or two longer.

17   St Andrews University in about 1800. ►

18   Oxbridge students were more interested in enjoying themselves than in learning. This satirical drawing shows a student suffering from "Headington Fever" — an overdose of enjoyment.
▼

You need not interrupt your amusements . . . we shall stop until we have the pleasure of your company.

If this was the attitude of the universities to mathematics, it is not surprising that one father who wanted his son to enter banking from school was told:

He cannot come from thence [Eton] into a [bank] without being some months at school in London to learn to write and also Accounts.

All this was to change, however. As the middle class grew in numbers, wealth and influence, they started to alter things at the universities. They could not afford to have their sons spending their university years hunting, drinking, whoring and gambling as most Oxbridge students did. They tried to see that their sons got the education they had paid for and so standards of learning began to improve and discipline was tightened. A sign of this improvement was the foundation, in 1828, of London University, the first of many universities founded in the nineteenth century. Its main purpose was to educate and it gave opportunities to students from wider backgrounds. One of the founders, Henry Brougham, was a self-made Scottish lawyer, not one of the aristocracy, and it is largely due to the work of such "new" men that universities achieved the standing and respect they have today.

Education for girls

Girls from the better-off families received even less education than their brothers. Occasionally they might share their brothers' tutor, but more often they had a governess of their own. Governesses were usually daughters of once prosperous families which had fallen on hard times. With no money of their own, their chances of marriage were slight and the only respectable way of earning a living was by teaching, regardless of

19   The family governess, obviously finding her position gloomy.

whether they wanted to or were any good at it. The subjects a governess taught were not very demanding. Reading, writing, drawing and painting, French, music and sewing were, in general, all that it was thought necessary for girls to know and all that a governess had to teach. Unlike Jane Eyre, the character in Charlotte Brontë's novel, very few governesses married their employers. In reality a governess's position in a family was a difficult one because she was neither a servant nor a member of the family. She was despised by the servants and looked down upon by her employers and pupils.

20   A cartoon of a female academy, entitled "The Scholastic Hen and her Chickens". The caption explained that the mistress, Miss Thimblebee, is saying: "Turn your heads the other way my dears for here are two horridly handsome officers coming."

24

Female academies

There were some "female academies" which charged high fees for teaching the daughters of the wealthy. French, singing, music and dancing figured largely in the syllabus of such establishments. A famous cartoon of the time shows the salon of one of these academies. It suggests that, with all the handsome young officers hanging about, the girls learnt rather more than their parents intended!

Education for the poor — Sunday schools

The general attitude to education for poor children was summed up by John Byng who, opposing Sunday schools, wrote:

> I am point-blank against these institutions; the poor should not read, and of writing I never learnt, for them, the use.

This opinion prevailed for many years, and things were slow to change. By 1825, however, most large towns had Mechanics' Institutes, where interested adult workers could attend lectures and read books in the library. Also the Society for the Diffusion of Useful Knowledge was established to provide cheap books for the workers. Although such measures were well-intentioned, it was up to the individual adult to make the effort to use them. It was still many years before the right of all children to have an education, whatever their background, was acknowledged.

During the Industrial Revolution the only way a poor child could receive any sort of education was through the charity of better-off members of society. Charitable people formed voluntary societies which set up charity schools. These were held on Sundays — the only day when poor children were not working. In fact, the people who set up these schools seemed less interested in giving the children a real education than in getting the children off the streets, making them wash and teaching them about religion. But at least the children probably learnt to read and write, whereas children in an area where there was no voluntary society for the education of the poor had very little chance of learning even this.

One of the pioneers of the Sunday schools movement was Robert Raikes, the owner of

Noses to the North!

the newspaper *The Gloucestershire Journal*. He described the effect that Sunday schools had on the children:

> From being idle, ungovernable, profligate, and filthy in the extreme, they say the boys and girls are become not only cleanly and decent in appearance, but are greatly humanised in their manners — more orderly, tractable and attentive to business.

For the businessmen of the times those last seven words were the crux of the matter, for docile children made docile workers.

Another supporter of the Sunday schools was Jedidiah Strutt. When he opened a Sunday school for his workers at Belper, he received extravagant praise from the local paper, *The Derby Mercury*:

> Liberality which does Honour to the human Heart . . . . It becomes the Duty of every thinking Person in this Age of Refinement, Luxury, and Vice, to hold forth an assisting Hand, to stop the Tide of Immorality, which threatens speedily to Deluge "The Land of Liberty".

These comments are also interesting for the light they throw on social attitudes at the time.

Ragged schools

Also at the end of the eighteenth century the ragged schools were started. They too attempted to deal with the problems of deprived children. The first ragged school was started by John Pounds, a Portsmouth cobbler. He took in children who had no home, no family and no work. He taught them to read and write, to cook their food and mend their clothes. It seems very little, but the alternative for such children was a life of thieving, begging and prostitution (Chapter 9). Pounds' work was copied by others and slowly spread. Eventually it grew into the important and influential Ragged and Industrial Schools movement of the later nineteenth century.

Once children attending these schools had learnt to read, they needed "suitable" books. This provided the reformers with a splendid opportunity to continue their moralizing approach to educating the under-privileged. One social reformer, Hannah More, wrote that "to teach the poor to read without providing them with safe books has always

21 Brook Street Ragged and Industrial School. The monitorial system of teaching is being used. On the wall on the right two posters read "Be sure your sins will find you out" and "That the soul be without knowledge is not good".

appeared to me as a dangerous measure". Accordingly she wrote large numbers of "safe" books. Among them were *The Roguish Miller*, who cheated his customers but was jailed in the end, and *The Story of Sinful Sally*, who read too many novels. Her ballad, *The Riot, or Half a Loaf is Better than no Bread*, was said to have helped prevent riots for bread during the great shortages in 1795.

The monitor system

Many of the voluntary schools were run on the monitor system — a popular method of teaching, by which one person could teach a large number of pupils. The master gave a lesson to a group of the oldest boys, or monitors. Then the rest of the pupils were divided into groups and a monitor was put at the head of each. He had to teach the younger boys what he himself had just learnt. Discipline at these schools was strict. As the headmaster of a school in Bermondsey remarked: "It is kept by word of command, just as in His Majesty's [George III's] army". Undoubtedly the "word of command" he spoke of was backed by the belt or birch if necessary. This was a reflection of society's attitude in general — the poor should know their place and be kept there by force if they forgot it.

Factory schools

Some of the more enlightened industrialists, like Richard Arkwright and Robert Owen, built schools beside their mills and factories and employed a teacher for the children. But such men were few, and the children were generally too tired from their hard work in the factory to benefit. Indeed, the provision in the 1833 Factory Act for children under thirteen to receive two hours' education a day was soon dropped as impracticable. The children commonly worked a 48-hour week, which was brought up to sixty hours by the extra two hours of school each day. Even the hard taskmasters of the time agreed that this was too much. And anyway, the important work — the work in the factory — might suffer.

Dame schools

The children of small tradesmen and shopkeepers went to dame schools. For a halfpenny or two a week the elderly ladies who ran these schools passed on what little learning they had to their pupils. Many of them were no more than childminders, but at least they kept the children from roaming the streets. In his poem "The Borough", published in 1810, George Crabbe described one of these schools:

> To every class we have a school assign'd,
> Rules for all ranks, and food for every mind:
> Yet one there is, that small regard to rule
> Or study pays, and still is deemed a school;
> That, where a deaf, poor, patient widow sits,
> And awes some thirty infants as she knits;
> Infants of humble, busy wives, who pay
> Some trifling price for freedom through the day.

This scene was repeated in countless towns and villages throughout the country.

22   Children at a dame school.

5 Work in the Country

In the early days of the Industrial Revolution Britain's economy was still firmly based on agriculture. The country was self-sufficient in food, except for sugar, which had to be imported. And corn was even exported from Britain to Europe. The majority of the population still lived in the country and were employed in agriculture — which was still very labour-intensive. Farmers, traditionally conservative in their ways, continued to use farming methods which had been used for many generations.

However, changes were beginning, thanks to the pioneering work of men like Thomas Coke and Robert Bakewell, who did much to improve the quality of crops and stock. While these improvements still had little immediate effect on the majority of the population, there was one change linked to them which had an enormous effect on life in the country — the enclosures.

23   Reaping. Without machinery, agriculture was labour-intensive.

Enclosures

The system of enclosures now forced many farmers out of their traditional livelihood. Enclosures had occurred spasmodically since Elizabeth I's reign (1558-1603). Until then families who worked for a landowner used to rent from him a number of narrow strips of land scattered in different parts of the farm. With this system, going from one strip to another wasted a lot of time and weeds from a neglected strip soon spoilt the neighbouring ones. And so individual tenants sometimes made arrangements with each other to consolidate their scattered strip holdings into one compact block. The land was then enclosed with a rough fence or hedge, to prevent other people's animals from eating or trampling their crops. Farming became a little more efficient with these enclosures, but they were only small-scale. Gradually, however, more people began to see the advantages of the new system of land-holding. Landlords reorganized their estates, preferring to have fewer tenants holding more land than before. Rent-collecting became easier. The landlords also preferred to arrange leases of a maximum twenty years, so that a neglectful tenant could be more easily removed.

In the eighteenth century enclosures increased. At first they were achieved by individual, local negotiations and pressure. In the second half of the century they were enforced by Act of Parliament after the landowner, often an MP or member of the House of Lords, had presented a petition requesting the change. There was some attempt at justice. Surveyors were appointed to oversee the changes, and although some were quite openly corrupt, giving the most land to whoever payed the biggest bribe, many tried to apportion the land fairly.

But for many tenant farmers and their labourers the result of the enclosures was that they were left with no livelihood in the country, and so they drifted to the growing towns where they hoped to get a job at one of the new factories.

The enclosures affected the lives of those who stayed in the country too, of course. As enclosures were arranged or enforced, a yeoman farmer usually received a compact holding of about 12 hectares (30 acres) of land. According to the new system, the boundaries had to be hedged or fenced. This was very expensive and so often only the outer boundary was fenced, while the field divisions within the small farm were simply marked out by a few rough stakes or a narrow strip of unploughed land.

24   "Turnip Townshend".

People were less well off than they had been. When common land around a village was enclosed, families had nowhere to keep their animals. As a result, the amount of meat and dairy produce in the diet of most country people, and that was the majority, went down considerably.

Fertilizers and rotation
Earlier generations of farmers had understood little about the importance of fertilizing fields and rotating crops so as not to exhaust the soil. Usually they just grew a different crop for two years and in the third year left the ground fallow. That is, they planted no crop at all for a year, allowing the grass (and weeds) to grow and the land to rest. It was a wasteful system and, particularly as the population grew and more people had to be fed, a new method needed to be found, using all the land all the time. Eighteenth-century farmers, led by the 2nd Viscount Townshend ("Turnip Townshend")

used the Norfolk system. This meant growing four crops in rotation — turnips, barley or oats, clover and wheat. This balance of crops actually helped to improve the land.

Also, in the eighteenth century, much more use was made of fertilizers than before. In particular, marl, a soil consisting of clay and lime, was used. In areas like East Anglia the old marl pits can still be seen at the edges of fields.

New machines
New machines for farming included the horsedrill and the horsehoe. These had been invented by Jethro Tull in the early years of the eighteenth century, but had met much opposition. The drill, which sowed seeds automatically at regular intervals, caused a

25 The first horsehoe was invented by Jethro Tull at the beginning of the eighteenth century. This is one of many developments of it.

labourers' strike when it was introduced. They said that seed should be scattered broadcast as described in the Bible. However, by the end of the Industrial Revolution both machines were becoming fairly commonly used.

The new methods of farming increased crop yields but were more expensive than the old. The small farmer could not afford the machinery and fertilizers required for the new methods. In the meantime those who could afford them were able to sell their increased yields of crops at a cheaper price. Unable to compete, the smaller yeomen farmers had to sell their holdings and face the prospect, if they were lucky, of becoming tenants of their former landlord. Otherwise, they would have to become employees on one of his farms.

The farm labourers disliked the machines because they reduced the number of workers needed on the farms. Children were still useful to scare away the birds during the sowing of crops, but the women and teenage girls who had usually made up the teams who weeded the fields, were replaced by the horsehoe in many areas. This in turn reduced the income of the families of agricultural workers.

Livestock

The successful experiments in livestock breeding carried out by Coke and Bakewell also had the effect of reducing agricultural employment. For fields that had once needed ploughing, sowing, hoeing and harvesting were turned over to grazing land for the new, improved breeds. These included the New Leicester sheep bred by Bakewell on his estate at Dishley in Leicestershire and the shorthorn cows developed by the Collins brothers of Darlington.

Jobs for the children

Most country women and their daughters, when there was little to do in the fields, tended the family's garden, or took in outside work (Chapter 6). At the busy seasons of haymaking and harvest there was more than enough for all the family to do. Even the small children helped. Some took jugs of ale or bread and cheese to the fields for their parents' lunch. Others gleaned, picking up ears of corn which had fallen from the sheaves of grain that the men were bundling up. Gleaning was an important task because each family kept the corn they had gleaned. It was ground into flour for bread, and the less bread or flour that had to be bought the better, because it was both expensive and the staple part of the diet.

Women and girls also worked in the fields, like their fathers and brothers. Although they did not do the heaviest work like ploughing or reaping the corn, hoeing for eight hours or so a day and collecting big baskets of stones from off the fields was certainly not light work.

The dairy

The dairy was one area where women and girls did almost all the work. Milking the cows, separating out the cream, making butter and cheese were all jobs done by women. It is said that the lovely complexions of most dairymaids inspired Edward Jenner to experiment with smallpox inoculation in the late 1780s and 1790s. Dairymaids frequently got cowpox, a very mild disease related to the much more severe smallpox. At worst smallpox killed; at best it left its victims with badly scarred faces. But dairymaids having had cowpox rarely caught smallpox. In the words of the nursery rhyme "My face is my fortune, sir, she said".

Before roads and transport improved, most counties, and even quite small districts, had their own special cheeses. Among them were Stilton, Derby, Double-Gloucester, Lancashire, Cheddar and Cheshire. But many more have long since been forgotten, together with the women whose knowledge and skills were the result of generations of tradition.

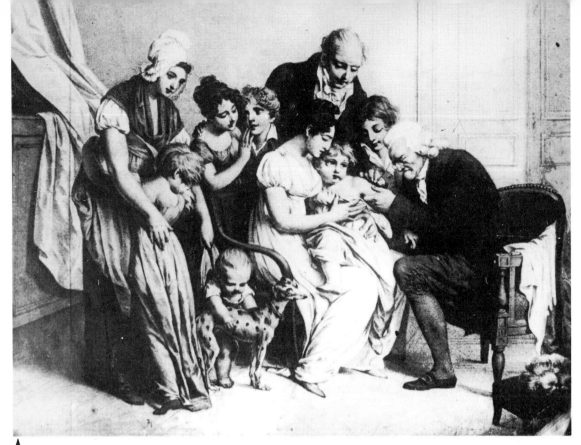

26   A painting of Edward Jenner inoculating a child against smallpox.

27   The cartoonist's view of inoculation against smallpox. It is captioned "The Cow-Pock — or — the Wonderful Effects of the New Inoculation!"

Work as a servant

Work was also available to girls and boys as servants in the home of one of the local gentry. Many servants were just as exploited as the labourers on the farms or the workers in the mills. In a small household they were commanded by their employer; in a large one they were at the mercy of the housekeeper who, with the butler, was the most senior and important of the servants.

However, domestic service was the only means by which a girl from a poor background could get on. By much hard work she might be able to work her way up through the various ranks of servant — maid of all work, under-maid, chambermaid and parlourmaid — to become a housekeeper. Then she could enjoy the status of having a sitting-room of her own and the courtesy title of "Mrs", whether or not she was married. But to achieve these heights meant years of hard, unrewarding work, often from the age of ten. Holidays were few, the pay ungenerous and, although the job included board and lodging, the food was not always sufficient and the servants' quarters were usually in damp basements or in tiny, cold attics at the top of the house.

28 A servant girl plucking a turkey. (Painting by Henry Walton, 1776.)

6 Cottage Industries

Until the coming of the factory system of manufacture, the products of many industries had been made in the homes of the workers.

29 Spinning flax at home. The woman outside is working her spindle by hand. The wheel indoors was "modern" by comparison.

These domestic or cottage industries were important both to the country and to the family doing the work. In fact, even with the great changes brought about by the Industrial Revolution, the domestic system of manufacture continued into the early nineteenth century.

The textile industry was particularly well suited to this type of manufacture. The general pattern was that while the men in a family worked for the local farmer or on the family's own land, the mother and daughters took in paid work from outside. Spinning and weaving work was available almost anywhere in the country in the days before water- and steam-powered machinery. There were local varieties of work too, like lace-making in Bedfordshire and stocking-knitting in Leicestershire and Nottinghamshire. An enterprising businessman bought the necessary raw material, usually cotton or wool, and then distributed it, to be woven or spun, to anyone in the neighbouring villages who wanted work. A week or so later he called round again to collect and pay for the finished work and to give out more raw material.

From a family's point of view it was an excellent system. They worked at home. When there was little or no work to be done on the land there was plenty of time for spinning and weaving and so boosting their income. Everyone in the family was involved. Even the smallest children soon learnt to pick thistles and burrs out of the wool as they carded it for their sisters to spin into thread.

Of course, there were some snags. The homes of most families who did this work were small and crowded anyway. The spinning wheels, knitting frames and hand looms made them even more crowded. But in an age when families were used to sharing a bed as well as the bedroom and personal privacy was a very rare luxury, the cramped homes did not worry people as they would today.

In Yorkshire, many farmers took wool

30 A lacemaker.

31 A scale model of a hand loom. Looms like this were kept in people's homes.

from their own sheep, spun and wove it into cloth which they then sold at the local market. They were truly independent manufacturers. Others were not so lucky. In Derby each Monday morning about 400 people from the surrounding villages gathered at Jedidiah Strutt's warehouse to collect their week's supply of yarn. The following Saturday afternoon they returned with the four pairs of stockings they had each made. They earned 2s 6d (12½p) per pair, but they had to rent the frame on which the stockings were made from Strutt, at a charge of one shilling (5p) per week.

Other industries geared to domestic

32   A boy working at a machine for fixing tags to laces.

production included, surprisingly, the metal trades for which Birmingham was becoming well known. Chains, locks, bolts, nails, buttons, buckles and pins were mostly made in small home workshops by women and children. It was said that the small, nimble fingers of children were most suited to the small items made in this way.

Another rather surprising cottage industry was pottery manufacture. In the area around Stoke-on-Trent known as the Potteries most

families had a pottery oven in their garden. These ovens were made out of turf, with a roof of branches, and they were heated by charcoal. Simple earthenware pots and jars were fired in them. Many of these pots and jars were used to transport goods like butter on the strings of packhorses, which were the chief means of transporting goods at this period before roads had improved.

Of course, the few heavy industries of the time, coal mining, shipbuilding and iron

33 Thorncliffe iron works, 1810. This was heavy industry, but the setting is still rural.

smelting, could never be carried out in this domestic way. But few things better illustrate the immense changes of this period than the fact that at the beginning most manufacturing production took place in the homes of the workers, whereas at the end it took place in purpose-built factories and mills to which the workers had to travel each day.

7 The Growth of Mills and Factories

Domestic industries could never be more than small-scale. Even Jedidiah Strutt, the Derbyshire stocking manufacturer, was restricted in expanding his highly successful business because his workers were not centralized in one place. His home workers lived within walking distance of his warehouse — which in fact meant many miles away because, as walking was the chief means of transport for the poor, they were used to covering much greater distances on foot than we would consider today. So, twice a week Strutt's home workers walked to his warehouse to collect raw material and return the

finished stockings. These journeys wasted potential manufacturing time, and furthermore, the employer had little control over his workers (except payment for finished work) when they worked in their own homes.

Small-scale industries had been sufficient for a small population since the demand for goods was also small. But as the population increased in numbers and in wealth, as it did during the Industrial Revolution, so the demand for goods also grew. Eventually industries organized on such a small scale and in so fragmented a way could not cope. Realizing that traditional methods of manufacture could not satisfy the demand for goods, enterprising businessmen now took existing technical knowledge and built on it to introduce new methods of production. In so doing they laid the foundations of today's industrial society and disrupted a pattern of living many generations old.

New machines

Actually, many new, improved forms of manufacture had been known for some time. For example, a frame for making stockings had been known as early as the reign of Elizabeth I, but it was apparently suppressed then so that it would not threaten jobs among the stocking makers. It was only when the demand for goods became too great for the traditional methods of manufacture that such inventions were adopted.

Even then the new machines did not always meet with the approval of the workers. The first, the Flying Shuttle, patented by John Kay as early as 1733, was really intended to speed up the weaving of woollen cloth. Weaving was a slow process. To weave one piece of cloth (unless it was to be a very narrow piece), two men were needed, sitting side by side at the loom, to pass the shuttle bearing the width-ways threads by hand to and fro between the length-ways threads. Kay's Flying Shuttle

34 Women in an early factory producing buttons.

passed much more quickly across the loom and it was worked by only one man pulling a cord. But when the machine was patented in 1733 the wool weavers feared that it would put them out of work. They broke into Kay's home at Bury, Lancashire, destroying his machines and property. Kay fled to France, where he is believed to have died in poverty. However, in the 1750s and 1760s his invention was adopted by the cotton industry, who recognized its advantages.

New machines caused new problems. The new looms were too large to fit into the cottages of the domestic workers. And so enterprising businessmen, with some capital to spare, built large weaving sheds to house the looms. The more they could cram into the sheds, the better for the industrialists. The noise and the over-crowding did not concern them, provided plenty of cloth to sell was produced. And it was. Indeed, the weavers now had the capacity to make more cloth than there was thread available from which to weave it.

A number of inventors then looked for a solution to the shortage of thread problem caused by the invention of the new looms. The most successful solution was James Hargreaves' Spinning Jenny, which he patented in 1770. Other spinners noticed how much more yarn he and his family produced. Jealous, they broke into his home in Blackburn and smashed the machines. Hargreaves moved to Nottingham and made improvements to his original design, which had been able to spin eight threads at once. Finally he developed a machine which spun 120 threads.

Arkwright's development of the water-powered spinning frame almost coincided with Hargreaves' Jenny. Other inventions and improvements followed and always met with resistance. Arkwright's property was attacked and some of his mills were burnt down by rioting workers who feared for their jobs. The machine-breakers were nick-named "Luddites", apparently after Ned

37 A mill in Scotland. This was the sort of ▶ building which amazed people by its size.

Ludd, a retarded boy who is said to have destroyed some stocking-frames in a fit of rage and frustration.

Mills

To start with, the new machines were worked by water power. Therefore the first of the big textile mills were built beside the swift-flowing streams of hilly areas like Yorkshire and the West Country. These mills became known as "beckside mills". They caused amazement, as few people had ever seen buildings so large before. The cotton-spinning mill built by Richard Arkwright at Cromford in Derbyshire in the early 1770s was described as "a palace of enormous size, having at least a score of windows in a row and five or six storeys in height".

▲
35 Arkwright's improved spinning machine or water frame. Compare this with the spinning wheel in picture 29.

36 James Hargreaves' Spinning Jenny.
▼

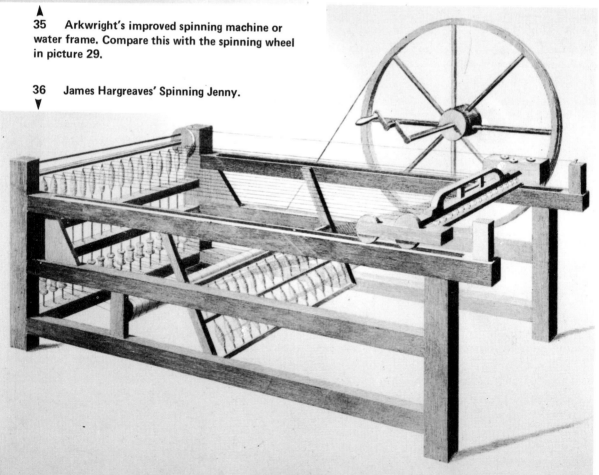

38   Sir Richard Arkwright.

The textile industry in the north-east of England flourished as Britain's trade increased with her growing number of overseas colonies. Indeed, this helped the economy of the whole country. Until the Industrial Revolution the north-west had always been a rather poor region. But now, as Liverpool, the port which served the region, expanded through its trade with the new colonies, the economy of the area expanded with it. One of the main items imported by the increasingly wealthy Liverpool merchants was

The fact that this early mill was for cotton is significant. Cotton was the most recent of the textile industries for which Britain was renowned. The others — wool, silk and linen — being longer established, were conservative about methods of manufacture.

Cotton goods had originally been imported from India, but because they were cheaper than other textiles they had been banned so as not to undercut the home industries. Until 1774 no 100-per-cent cotton goods could be sold, in case they were illegal imports from India. Perhaps all these restrictions made the cotton workers more enterprising than those in the other textile industries, for as early as in the 1720s they were experimenting with fabrics of cotton mixed with other fibres, such as linen, worsted and mohair.

39   A cotton mill, drawn in 1844. (Few drawings exist of an earlier date, for people took little interest in factory conditions until later.) On the left is a child who has crawled under the machine to pick up fluff or mend broken threads.

cotton from the West Indies. This reached the spinners and weavers of north-east Lancashire, bringing them more work. As a result, Manchester grew from an unimportant village in the 1720s to a city of more than 100,000 people by 1800.

Effects of the new system of working
The age of machines and factories had arrived. No mobs could stop them. The new methods of manufacturing had an enormous effect on people's home life. Women and children could no longer work at home. They now had to walk to the nearest mill, often several miles away, leaving home early in the morning and getting back tired out late in the evening. So, there was even less home life for the family. The cottage garden where fruit and vegetables had been grown by the mother to make up the family's diet became overgrown and neglected because she was now too tired to do anything about it.

In the end, of course, the new system of

manufacturing increased the number of jobs available. Its more immediate effect was to turn a large part of the population for the first time into regular wage-earners. Several of the more enlightened chroniclers of the time regretted that the once proudly independent Englishman had become an employee. And Oliver Goldsmith, in his rather exaggerated poem, "The Deserted Village", lamented the destruction of a "bold peasantry, their country's pride".

Employment of children

It was not just the adults who went out to work. Arkwright's advertisement when he opened his second mill at Cromford read:

Filing Smiths, Joiners and Carpenters, Framework knitters and weavers with large families. Likewise children of all ages above 7 years old, may have constant employment.

40   Children leaving the factory, 1805. This is a rather idealized picture. People were slow to realize the horror of factory conditions. But in the early days the mills and factories were in pleasant country surroundings.

Men were only needed to build the mills and set up the machinery. After that, women and children were best — from the employer's point of view. They were cheaper to hire, less likely to argue with the overseer, and more nimble-fingered. The further great advantage of child workers was that they were small enough to crawl under the machines — while they were still working — to pick up fluff and dirt and to mend any threads that had broken. Children had worked before, of course. But there was a big difference between helping out when the family worked at home and working in a factory for ten hours a day with probably only two half-hour breaks for meals.

When the supply of local children was exhausted, the mill-owners had batches of pauper children sent up from London from the workhouses (Chapter 9). While still young, these pauper apprentices were sure of employment, but once grown-up, they usually lost their jobs. That, however, was a problem which many of them did not have to face, because they were dead before then.

Children who worked in the factories and their parents were interviewed about their lives for a Commission on Factory Children's Labour in 1831:

"At what time in the morning, in the brisk [busiest] time, did these girls go to the mills?" "In the brisk time, about six weeks, they have gone at 3 o'clock in the morning, and ended at 10 or nearly half past ten at night."
"What intervals were allowed for rest or meals during the nineteen hours of labour?" "Breakfast a quarter of an hour, and dinner half an hour, and drinking [a teabreak] a quarter of an hour."
"Was any of that time taken up in cleaning the machinery?" "They generally had to do what is called drying down. Sometimes this took the whole of the time at breakfast or drinking, and they were to get their dinner or breakfast how they could . . ."
"Had you not great difficulty in awakening your children to this excessive labour?" "Yes, in the early time we had to take them up asleep and shake them and dress them, before we could get them off to their work . . ."
"What was the length of time they could be in bed during those long hours?" "It was near 11 o'clock before we could get them into bed after getting them a little victuals [food] . . ."
"What time did you get them up in the morning?" "In general me or my missus got up at 2 o'clock to dress them."
"So that they had not above four hours sleep at this time?" "No they had not."
"For how long did this last?" "About six weeks, it was only done when the throng [rush] was very much on."
"The common hours of labour were from six in the morning until half-past eight at night?" "Yes."
"With the same intervals for food?" "Yes, just the same."
"What were the wages in the short hours?" "Three shillings [15p] a week each."
"When they worked those very long hours what did the children get?" "Three shillings and sevenpence halfpenny [18½p]."

Robert Owen

Not all industrialists were bad employers, however. Robert Owen (1771-1858), a self-made manufacturer, was a particularly good one. He set up in business in 1799 and working conditions in his factories at New Lanark, outside Glasgow, were better than in most others. He also built a village for his workers near the mills. The houses were better built and larger than the usual, cheap-as-possible housing put up by the majority of industrialists (Chapter 3). He opened a school for the

41   Robert Owen.

children at New Lanark, believing that everyone, however humble their background, should have the opportunity to learn to read and write.

Truck shops

Robert Owen also abolished the trucking system in the shops in his villages. This was a particularly mean and hated form of exploitation, dating from the days when many factories were in isolated areas. The employer paid his workers with special tokens instead of proper money. The tokens could only be exchanged at a few shops, where the prices were exorbitantly high because the shopkeeper knew that the poor workers could not spend their "money" anywhere else. And, in fact, as the shops belonged to the factory-owner, the system was simply a way for him to make even more money.

Robert Owen's ideas and improvements made him unpopular with his fellow industrialists, especially as his factories were extremely successful. Far more factory-owners supported Arthur Young's opinion that

> Everyone but an idiot knows that the lower classes must be kept poor or they will never be industrious.

42   Steam-powered cotton factories in Manchester, 1829.

They argued that to raise wages would increase production costs, and so prices would have to rise. This would then reduce demand and in turn lead to unemployment. Therefore the workers would be no better off.

Steam comes to the factories

The steam engine had been used in coal and tin mines for some years (see page 51). In the 1780s a farsighted mill-owner realized its potential for the textile industry. It was probably the clergyman, Edmund Cartwright, because in 1789 his Doncaster factory was fitted with a steam engine. Two years later a Manchester company ordered several steam-powered looms — the beginning of an inevitable trend that increased in momentum throughout the Industrial Revolution.

Water-powered textile mills were idle for many of the summer months, because there was not enough water in the streams to drive the machinery. Steam-powered machinery made continuous, regular work possible. This was a great change for people used to an agricultural economy. For centuries work

43   The aqueduct over the river Irwell.

46

had been dictated by the seasons of the year. The bustle of the spring and summer months, with their sowing, haymaking and harvesting, was followed by the long, bleak autumn and winter period when there was little work to be done. Then many agricultural workers were used to eking out their income by taking in work to do in their own homes (Chapter 6). Working like this, they were independent. Working long, monotonous, regular hours all through the year for the mill-owners, they were not.

The siting of the steam-powered mills and factories caused more suffering. At least, when the mills were worked by water power, they were usually in pleasant country districts, where the air outside was fresh. But mills using steam-powered looms had to be near coalfields. In such areas new factories were built and narrow streets of cheap housing were put up by the industrialists for their workers (Chapter 3). By the end of the Industrial Revolution, the majority of children lived and, all too often, died in such towns.

Reactions to the factories

The new industries and their products were regarded as marvellous by those who did not have to live or work among them. In 1759 James Brindley's aqueduct, 12.2 metres (40 feet) above the river Irwell, was built to carry coal from the Duke of Bridgewater's collieries at Worsley to the river Mersey. Arthur Young, who travelled all round England at this time and wrote an account of what he saw, described the aqueduct as "exceeding the noblest work of the Romans when masters of the world". (The Romans had also built aqueducts — of stone, not iron.) Young was not the only person impressed by the outward signs of the Industrial Revolution's progress. The Reverend John Dalton celebrated a visit to a coal mine with a poem. He ended it by praising Thomas Savery (page 51) who had first patented an engine to pump water from the mines:

Men's richest gift thy work will shine,
Rome's aqueducts were poor to thine.

But, as the more obvious effects of industry became visible in the countryside, the factories came to be thought of as "dark satanic mills" — a far cry from Roman aqueducts! William Blake's poem "Jerusalem" is an attack on all that was outwardly unpleas-

ant about the Industrial Revolution. And, as early as 1803, Henry Kirke White did not like what he saw of Nottingham, even though it was from a distance:

> . . . where the town's blue turrets dimly rise,
> And manufacture taints the ambient skies,
> The pale mechanic leaves the labouring loom,
> The air-pent hold, the pestilential room . . .

The effects of industry on the people employed in it were less apparent, particularly to those who did not wish to see — and that was practically everybody who was not involved. It was many years before a few enlightened reformers realized what the factory system was doing to other human beings.

Reformers

One early reformer was Sir Robert Peel, a Manchester mill-owner and father of the future great Victorian prime minister. His lobbying helped to get the first factory act passed — the Health and Morals of Apprentices Act of 1802. This stated that no apprentice was to work longer than twelve hours a day, and that no apprentice was to do any work at night. In addition, factories were to be white-washed inside and have proper ventilation. The apprentices were to be given better clothes and sleeping accommodation. They were also to receive a little elementary education.

The Act failed because it was to be enforced by the local Justices of the Peace who had powers to inspect the factories — and the JPs were often the mill-owners themselves, or their friends. But although there was little chance of the Act's being enforced properly, a body of opinion was slowly building up which was to lead to the passing of the effective Factory Act of 1833.

The greatest reformer of the time, and certainly the one who did the most for children, was Anthony Ashley Cooper, 7th Lord Shaftesbury (1801-85), whose name

and work are still remembered in the Shaftesbury Society. He and other humane industrialists stirred consciences and collected evidence of what they regarded as the evils of the factory system. One Tory land agent, Richard Oastler, said that the "Yorkshire Slavery" in the factories was quite as bad as the slavery in the British colonies which Parliament was in the process of abolishing.

At last a Commission on Factory Children's Labour was set up in 1831. (Part of it

is quoted on page 45.) Its findings were published and provoked fierce debate in public and in Parliament. Finally the Factory Act of 1833 was passed. According to this law, no children under 9 years of age were to work in the factories at all. Those between 9 and 13 were only to work nine hours a day. And those of 13 to 18 were to work no longer than twelve hours a day. Children of under 13 were to receive two hours' education each day (Chapter 4). Four salaried factory inspectors were to be appointed to ensure that the Act was obeyed. This last clause was really the most important one. Although parents could, and did, lie about their children's ages, so that they could start working and earning before they were nine years old, factory-owners could no longer ignore the law as they had in 1802.

44   One of George Cruickshank's cartoons satirizing the reluctance of the government to introduce reforms of any sort.

8 Down the Mines

The coal-mining industry expanded enormously during the Industrial Revolution. There had, of course, been a mining industry for many years. As early as 1200, coal was being exported from Newcastle. But mining had only been on a small scale. The mines were open-cast and really little more than deep pits. The demand for coal slowly increased over the centuries, especially as its advantages for smelting iron ore and heating homes were recognized. Previously the only way to smelt iron ore was with charcoal. Britain's growing military power increased demand for the metal and this, in turn, increased the demand for charcoal. This put immense pressure on timber supplies, because it took two loads of wood to make one of

charcoal and two loads of charcoal to smelt one ton of ore. Although it is impossible to make precise estimates, it is thought that about 6 million tons of coal were produced during the years 1700-70, 16 million tons between 1770 and 1816 and, in the twenty years from 1816 to 1836, about 30 million tons. A quite incredible increase in an unmechanized industry!

As the coal industry grew, the coal in the shallow open-cast pits was soon exhausted and so the miners had to go down deeper. They went down further, working outwards from the bottom of a shaft 9 to 12 metres

45 Bradley Mine, Staffordshire. The unprotected lamps might cause explosions.

(30-40 feet) deep, leaving great pillars of coal to support the rocks under which they were mining. In this way they wasted a lot of good coal. By the 1770s it was obvious that even deeper pits would be necessary and in some places depths of 180 metres (600 feet) had already been reached. Such pits posed great problems for the technology of the time. There was the ever-present danger not only of gas, but also of flooding.

As early as in 1698 Thomas Savery had patented "an engine to raise water by fire" — a crude form of steam-driven pump to get water out of the mines. In 1711 Thomas Newcomen patented an improved form of this engine which was soon being used in many coal and tin mines. It was not very efficient because it used a lot of fuel, but even so it developed 5½ horsepower and could lift 50 gallons of water a minute from a depth of 35 metres (115 feet). And so miners could go deeper than before.

46 Matthew Boulton's Soho engineering works, where James Watt's steam engines were produced.

James Watt (1736-1819), a self-educated Scotsman, was the first to see that the steam engine could be an efficient source of power and he set out to establish it as such. He had difficulty finding anyone to put up the money for his work, as he had no rich or influential relations. Despairing of success, he worked as a surveyor of the cutting of one of the new canals. In Birmingham for his work, he met Matthew Boulton, head of the Soho Engineering Works in Birmingham and one of the most go-ahead businessmen of the day. The two men formed a partnership. Watt's steam engine, which was a development of Newcomen's design, was patented in 1769. In 1775 it finally went into production at Matthew Boulton's works. Later in the same year the first of Watt's engines was set up in a colliery near Birmingham.

An old-fashioned mine
A good description of a mine in the early years of the Industrial Revolution was given by William Howitt, writing in 1838 about his

boyhood in Derbyshire at the beginning of the nineteenth century:

I first saw the coal-pits at night. As I rode over a hill I suddenly perceived before me, in every direction, strange lights, that only seemed to make the darkness deeper. Melancholy sounds, as of groans and sighings, and wild lamentings, came upon my ear . . . . I could perceive by the fires, that blazed here and there in a hundred places . . . a wild landscape. . . . It was the coal-pits, that these fires were burning by them; and the sounds I heard were the sounds of the machinery by which the coal was drawn up, and of the steam-engines by which the pits were cleared of water.

Intrigued by this strange place, William returned in daylight:

I found that the smothered fires . . . were coke fires; that is fires in which they burn the soft coal to coke or mineral charcoal, in the same way that in forests they burn wood into charcoal. . . . I found the pits awful circular gulphs of some yards wide, and of an immense depth — some sixty or seventy yards [55-64 metres], others as much as 200 yards [183 metres].

Derbyshire was quite an important coal-mining district and William recognized that:

these were very old-fashioned pits. They were not worked by steam-engines. . . . They were worked only by a huge wheel, with one end of its axle on the earth and the other fixed on the beam above. This wheel . . . was turned round by a couple of horses; and a large rope uncoiling one way as it coiled the other round the wheel drew up the coal, and let down the chain for more at the same time.

Someone stood at the edge of the pit-shaft to pull the full coal-bucket to one side for emptying. It was a dangerous job:

At one of these pits a girl [did this job], and missing her foot as she approached the pit mouth to hook the load of coal, plunged headlong into the pit and was dashed to pieces.

Saddest of all, the person who heard her scream and reached her dead body first was her father, one of the miners.

William made friends with some of the miners and one day plucked up the courage to go down the mine.

I was arrayed in a flannel frock, such as the colliers all wear, lent me by a pit-boy, and a round crowned hat without brim, well stuffed with hay. In this guise a collier seated himself on the chain, and taking me on his knee, we were swung off over the pit-mouth . . . . Down we went. Around us gushed water from the bricks which lined the side of the pit and fell with a dreary splashing sound far, far below.

Children in the mines

As William commented, the mine he visited was relatively old-fashioned. As the industry expanded it demanded more workers, just like the growing textile industry. And again, women and children were regarded as the best employees. Although not as strong as men, they were cheaper, more docile and the children could crawl about the mines more quickly and easily than the adults. As some of the mine tunnels were only 45 centimetres high, this was an important consideration.

In the early days of the Industrial Revolution, whole families worked together in the mines, like the father and daughter William Howitt mentioned. This practice gradually

47   A trapper. ►

died out and, again as in the textile industry, large numbers of pauper children were brought in to the mines from elsewhere.

One of the worst jobs down the mines was that of the trapper. The youngest children, usually about six years old, had this task, because they were not yet big or strong enough to carry or pull anything. Instead, they sat beside a wooden trap-door (from which the job got its name), opening and closing it to let the coal trucks through. It was one of the easier jobs perhaps, but they were alone in the dark for a good twelve hours each day. Frequently they fell asleep, slumped across the track on which the coal trucks ran and were run over and killed or severely injured.

Descriptions of life in the mines by children who worked in them are recorded in a report which was published just after our period in 1843. According to seven-year-old Thomas Straw, who worked in the pits at Ilkeston, Derbyshire, he was not allowed to sleep in the pit or stand still. He always felt very tired and when he got home he had his tea and went straight to bed. Eight-year-old John Hawkins agreed. He, too, was too tired to play. His back and legs ached so much that he would rather have gone to school than down the mines.

Seventeen-year-old John Bostock had worked in the pits for many years. He was often so tired that on the way home he just lay down in the road. Many times his mother had to come and find him and half carry him to their wretched home, where she then had to feed him, because he was too tired even to eat his meal. This point was made over and over again by parents whose children worked in the mines: when the children did get home they were far too tired to eat. And the meal would have been little more than bread and soup, certainly not enough for anyone doing hard physical work.

John Leadbeater, an eighteen-year old who worked in the pit at Babbington, described how he had to walk two miles to the pit each day, to get there by six o'clock each morning. If he was lucky he finished at eight in the evening — a fourteen-hour day. Quite frequently he had to work all night and then do an ordinary day's work the following day.

Many of the adult miners and the children's parents did not like the work their children

had to do, but there was no alternative. Work and, therefore, money were scarce and every penny any member of a family could earn was needed in the constant struggle to make ends meet.

John Beasley, a 49-year-old miner working in the Shipley pit, told the parliamentary commissioners compiling the report how he had seen children "who could not get home without their father's assistance, and have fallen asleep before they could be put into bed". According to him, children were not strong enough to do any work in the mines until they were about eight or nine years of age, and even then should not work the same long hours that the men worked:

> The children are obliged to work at night if the waggon-road [on which the coal trucks ran] is out of repair, or the water is coming on them. It happens sometimes two or three times in the week. They then go down at six p.m. to six a.m. and have from ten minutes to half an hour allowed for supper.

He, himself, had worked continuously for thirty-six hours while still a child, and so had many of his friends.

Accidents in the mines

All forms of mine accidents were frequent. The only protection a miner had against falling rock or coal was the hay-stuffed hat mentioned by William Howitt. The people who first tried to reform the mining industry and improve the conditions of the miners estimated that as many as two thousand people each year were killed in pit accidents. Accidents happened very easily in the cold, dark and wet mine tunnels and shafts. If a boy or woman pulling the coal cart up a slope lost their footing and slipped, the cart ran backwards over the boys who were pushing it from behind. The tunnels were so narrow that there was no room for them to jump clear of the heavy truck.

Getting the coal to the surface was another problem. Some mines, like the one described by William Howitt, had horse-driven winding gear to raise the coal from the deep mines to the surface. Others did not. Then the women and children had to carry the coal out. They had to climb to the surface up a series of ladders with the coal in

48 Lord Shaftesbury visiting the coal mines to collect evidence in support of reform.

49   Dragging a coal cart.

baskets strapped to their backs. Sometimes the strap slipped or broke and the coal fell out onto those climbing up behind them. Many women and children lost their lives doing this work.

Even when the colliery had winding gear there was still a problem: finding a rope strong enough to stand the strain of raising heavy coal baskets many hundred feet. Frequently the ropes broke, sending the coal

50   Women carrying coal out of the mine.

buckets crashing down on those below. The winding gear was also used to lower the workers into the pit, and there was always the fear that the rope would break then, sending the miners to certain death. The problem was not really effectively overcome until 1839, when the wire cable was invented.

Lighting the mines was particularly difficult. Frequent explosions occurred, caused by the build-up of gases. Explosions would bring down the inadequately supported tunnel roofs, leaving many people trapped to die of hunger and suffocation. From 1815 Davy safety lamps were used in the mines. These were invented by Sir Humphry Davy (1778-1829), one of Britain's leading scientists. The lamps, which were an efficient source of light, had a shield to prevent the flame coming into contact with the explosive mine gases. Davy safety lamps did much to reduce accidents in the mines. They were still being used in British mines in the 1920s.

Early in the nineteenth century reformers insisted that there should be a coroner's inquest after every mine accident in the north of England. This was one of the first steps achieved towards improving conditions in the mines. Until then no inquest was held after an accident, however many people had died. This meant that the mine-owners had little reason to keep the mine gear safe or in good working order. If an accident happened as a result of their laziness or meanness, it was not made public and so there was little possibility of their being blamed. They could go on putting their employees' lives at risk. Compulsory inquests were a great step forward.

51   Two children are let down into a mine.

52   Mining with a Davy lamp.

9 Chimney Sweeps and Mudlarks

The population of Britain grew rapidly from the middle of the eighteenth century. More and more people were living in the unhealthy atmosphere of industrial towns. In view of their living conditions and the lack of adequate health care (Chapter 3), it is surprising that increasing numbers of children were surviving into adulthood. Thus there were more adults to have families and then more children who were likely to grow up and have children of their own.

Although industry expanded, bringing more employment with it, there was still not enough employment for the growing population. And so the number of poor people increased too. They were particularly hard hit by the Corn Law of 1815. Under this law, wheat could not be imported until it reached 80s (£4) a quarter. Although it was an attempt to protect farmers (and so their workers) against cheap imported grain flooding the market and undercutting the home-grown crop, in practice it just forced up the price of bread to exorbitant levels in years of poor harvest. On a weekly wage of 12s (60p), 3s (15p) for a 4lb (2 kilo) loaf was a lot of money to pay for a staple item of the family diet.

There was poverty in the countryside, especially in years of bad harvest, but far worse was the poverty in the fast-growing industrial towns. And it was the children, the weakest members in any society, who suffered most.

Society made some effort to cope with the problem but in the early years of the Industrial Revolution the system used for helping the poor was still largely the one implemented by the Poor Law in the reign of Elizabeth I (1558-1603). That system had been based on the fact that the population was almost entirely static, most people spending all their life in the parish in which they were born. It was the responsibility of the local parish councils to support any poor people living within the boundaries of their parish and they levied a tax on the richer people there for this purpose. Any tramp or vagrant who turned up was sent swiftly on his way to the next parish, each council in turn trying to avoid dealing with the problem posed by such a person. This system of helping the poor had been workable when it started in the sixteenth century, but with the shift in the country's economy and changing patterns of employment, it broke down completely.

The Speenhamland System

In 1795 the well-meaning magistrates of Speenhamland in Berkshire devised a new system for dealing with the poor. This became widely adopted, especially in the southern and eastern counties of England but, as the period progressed, it came in for frequent criticism. One of the most common complaints was that it encouraged the poor to be idle by giving them money however much or little they worked. Under the Speenhamland System the wages of "every poor and industrious man" were to be made up by the parish according to the size of the family and the price of a loaf of bread — an early form of index-linking!

Like so many well-intentioned measures it did not turn out so well when put into practice. If the labourers were going to have their money made up by the parish, the farmers who employed them saw that they did not need to pay them a living wage to start with. Many took the chance not to. The system was resented both by those who had to pay the rates which funded it and by the poor who disliked receiving "charity" with its implication that they could not look after themselves. Nevertheless, during a period when corn prices rose alarmingly, it undoubtedly saved the lives of very many poor families.

The size of the problem is shown by the fact that the poor rates are estimated to have been £6,000,000 a year in the early part of the nineteenth century.

Workhouses

The poor dreaded being put into the parish workhouse, where they were given poor quality food and accommodation in return for doing menial work. It was the final degradation. The workhouses were strictly run, usually by contractors who intended to make as much money as possible out of doing so. In 1797 the rules of the Kendal workhouse included:

> That no person be allowed to smoke in their bed or in their rooms, upon pain of being put 6 hours in the dungeon. . . . Persons convicted of lying to be stood on stools in the most public place of the dining-room while the rest are at dinner, and have papers fixed to their breasts with these words written thereon "Infamous Lyar" and shall lose that meal.

◄ **53** A parish clerk, schoolmaster and sexton, Thomas Gregory of Toddington, Bedfordshire. The parish clerk would be involved with running the workhouse.

54 A drawing from *Oliver Twist* of Oliver in the workhouse, asking for more. ►

In 1763 Jonas Hanway began a survey of eleven London parishes. Jonas Hanway was a governor of the Foundling Hospital started in 1745 by Thomas Coram (who is still commemorated in the name of Coram Fields, London) and so he was confronted every day with the problems of poor children in London. In his survey he discovered that of the 291 children taken into the various parish workhouses in 1763, 256 had died by New Year 1766, such were the conditions in which the children had to live. Hanway remarked that

> Few persons accustomed to cleanly living can bear the stench or stand the survey of such misery.

In 1744 the parish officials in Shoreditch,

George Cruikshank

London, were "obliged to put 39 children . . . into 3 beds, by which means they contract disorders from each other". In Liverpool a Workhouse, Infirmary, Dispensary and Fever Hospital was built to cope with the problem of over-crowding. But this enlightened approach was, unfortunately, exceptional.

Pauper apprentices

Pauper children, who had usually been abandoned as babies, were kept in the workhouse or in an orphanage for the first years of their life. As often as not the children ran away from the harsh conditions of these places and went to live by their wits in the city underworld. But if they remained in the workhouse until they were seven they were then apprenticed to a tradesman until they were twenty-one. In theory, arranging such training for the children was to ensure that they would later be able to earn their own living. In fact, it was a way for the parish to pass on the responsibility, and expense, of looking after the children to someone else. When the northern mill-owners advertised for children to work in their mills, the workhouse guardians, the members of the voluntary committees who ran the workhouses, were only too glad to send away a batch of their children.

Apprentices were little more than slaves to their masters who practically owned them. They had no legal rights, and even if they had had, illiterate, hungry and terrified of being beaten yet again, they would not have known how to take advantage of any legal help. No wonder many apprentices ran away to join the floating, homeless population of street children. There was always the risk of being caught and punished, but as the cities grew and the population of street children grew with them, the chances of this decreased. Also, because there were plenty more pauper children in the workhouses to provide cheap labour, there was little incentive for a master to search for his runaway apprentices.

Chimney sweeps

More apprentice chimney sweeps ran away than apprentices of any other trade. Chimney sweeping was painful, dirty work and master sweeps had a reputation for cruelty. At first the bricks of the chimney rubbed the boy's hands, elbows and knees raw. Soot or salt was rubbed in to stop the bleeding and toughen the skin. Eventually the skin became so hard and calloused that it did not graze or bleed, but by then cancer or some other skin disease could have set in.

The sweep's job became even more difficult and unpleasant as the cities developed. As land prices increased houses became taller and narrower. The houses in the Georgian terraces of towns like London, Brighton and Bath, so much admired today, had equally tall narrow chimneys, up which only the smallest child could go. Climbing several storeys high in the dark, narrow and suffocatingly sooty atmosphere of the chimneys must have been a terrifying experience.

It was quite common for homeless children to be sold on the streets. In 1785 Hanway reported that

> Orphans who are in a vagabond state, or the illegitimate children of the poorest kind of people are said to be sold, that is their service for seven years is disposed of for 20 or 30 shillings [£1 or £1.50].

William Blake added to this picture in his "Songs of Innocence", published in 1789:

> *When my mother died I was very young,*
> *And my father sold me, while yet my tongue*
> *Could scarcely cry " 'Weep! 'Weep! 'Weep!"*
> *So your chimneys I sweep and in soot I sleep.*

Many children were sold in this way to master chimney sweeps, who sometimes took on as many as twenty-four orphan boys, forcing them to beg in the streets during the

55   A chimney sweep. ➤

summer when there was no work, and hiring them out for 5d or 6d (2 or 3p) a day in winter.

The use of climbing boys (there are no records of girls ever having to sweep chimneys) — as the little chimney sweeps were called — was not abolished until well after the Industrial Revolution. Charles Kingsley's book *The Water Babies*, in which chimney sweeping plays an important part, had a great success when it was published in 1863. But despite the public outcry it stirred up against the practice, it was not until twelve years later — in 1875 — that the practice was finally abolished.

Street children

There were many ways for the street children to earn a few pence in the large cities, but this was seldom enough for them to live on.

A French visitor to London in the 1820s remarked that a few steps from the wealthy streets there lived "half starved children with the bodies of skeletons covered only in rags".

In those days of horse-drawn transport and badly surfaced roads, children acted as crossing sweepers, clearing a path across the street so that richer people could avoid getting their feet or the hems of their long dresses too dirty. On a very good day a child might earn one shilling (5p) this way. Although wages and prices were much lower than today, this was still very little and would not buy much.

Many children were mudlarks. The rivers of England were the sewers of the country. Every type of rubbish and refuse was dumped into them. At every low tide the muddy foreshores of the Thames, Mersey, Trent and other big rivers swarmed with mudlarks — children who collected anything from the refuse which they could then sell for a few pence. Coal sold at one penny (½p) for 7 kilos, 2½ kilos of iron fetched one penny (½p), but bones were more profitable — 3 kilos sold for twopence (1p).

56 Crossing sweepers. The drawing is a Victorian one.

Many of the slum children had no real homes. They might sleep in the same doorway for a few weeks, but that was the nearest they came to having a permanent home. Instead they formed gangs and lived by stealing. Sometimes the gangs were organized by an adult, like Fagin in Charles Dickens' *Oliver Twist*. Although a successful professional thief could earn quite a good living, the unsuccessful one who was caught faced appalling punishments. It made no difference if the thief was a child. In 1833 a boy was hung for stealing twopence (1p) worth of paint.

57 A mudlark.

58 Oliver Twist is received by Fagin, leader of ►
the gang of child thieves.

George Cruikshank

Prisons

It was thought that prison acted as a deterrent and so stiff prison sentences were given even for trivial crimes. But it was wrong to think that this would prevent crime. People thought, if the punishment for stealing half a loaf was prison, they might as well steal a whole loaf, since the punishment was no different.

John Howard (1726-90) was one of the first people to realize the horrors and uselessness of prison. (His work is commemorated in the name of the Howard League for Penal Reform, a modern pressure group.) Another prison reformer was Elizabeth Fry.

She described Newgate Prison in 1814:

Nearly 300 women, sent there for every kind of crime, some not even tried, kept in two small rooms and two cells. They all sleep on the floor without bedding. In all this horror were some 70 children.

Throughout the country, behind the fine new streets and imposing merchants' mansions was another world, which few of the better-off acknowledged. This twilight world was all that most city-dwelling children during the Industrial Revolution knew, despite the Ragged Schools (Chapter 4) and the charitable efforts of individual people. The improvements that came later in the nineteenth century were too late for uncounted numbers of city children.

59 Elizabeth Fry.

10 A Look Back at the Changes

Many of the events and changes which took place during the Industrial Revolution and which have had an immense importance on the overall history of Britain passed unnoticed at the time by many people. People did not travel as they do today and there were no modern news media. For example, during the Napoleonic Wars, which raged for most of the period of the Industrial Revolution, it was feared that the French would invade England. But if such a national disaster as this had happened, the people in small market towns like Uttoxeter could only learn of it from the post boy, who might arrive before his weekly visit to bring their post was due. And so large areas of the country remained ignorant of events like the cutting of the canals, the Peterloo Massacre in 1819, the parliamentary disputes between Whigs and Tories, the great Reform Act of 1832 and the early railways.

But everyday life changed enormously too. One person who grew up during the Industrial Revolution was Sydney Smith. He became a clergyman and Dean of St Paul's. Just before he died in 1845 he looked back at some of the changes he had seen during his long life. Some of them have been mentioned in this book; others were still a few years off:

A young man, alive at this period [i.e. the 1840s], hardly knows to what improvements of human life he has been introduced; and I would bring to his notice [some] changes which have taken place in England since I first began to breathe in

60 Sydney Smith.

61 Gas lighting was an invention of the Industrial Revolution period, as Sydney Smith remarked. This cartoon shows sarcastically "One of the Advantages of Gas over Oil". ▶

64

One of the Advantages of GAS over OIL.

66

the breath of life — a period now amounting to nearly seventy-three years. Gas was unknown: I groped about the streets of London in all but the utter darkness of a twinkling oil lamp . . .

I have been nine hours in sailing from Dover to Calais before the invention of steam. It took me nine hours to go from Taunton to Bath, before the invention of rail roads, and I now go in six hours from Taunton to London! In going from Taunton to Bath, I suffered between 10,000 and 12,000 severe contusions, before stone-breaking Macadam was born. I paid £15 in a single year for repairs of carriage-springs on the pavements of London; and I now glide without noise or fracture on wooden pavements.

I can walk, by the assistance of the police, from one end of London to the other, without molestation . . .

I had no umbrella! They were little used and very dear. There were no water-proof hats . . . I could not keep my small clothes in their proper place, for braces were unknown. If I had gout there was no colchicum. If I was bilious there was no calomel. If I was attacked by ague there was no quinine . . . . The corruptions of Parliament, before Reform, were infamous. There were no banks to receive the savings of the poor. The Poor Laws were gradually sapping the vitals of the country; and, whatever miseries I suffered, I had no post to whisk my complaints for a single penny to the remotest corners of the empire . . .

I forgot to add that, as the basket of stage-coaches, in which luggage was then carried had no springs, your clothes were rubbed all to pieces; and that even in the best society one third of the gentlemen at least were always drunk.

62   The opening of the Stockton-Darlington Railway, 1825. The artist had little idea of how the train worked apparently. The wheels of the trucks do not seem to be running on anything!

Date List

1760	George III comes to the throne
1769	James Watt patents his steam engine
1770	Spinning Jenny patented by James Hargreaves
1775	Alexander Cummings patents a water closet
1775	James Watt and Matthew Boulton form business partnership to manufacture Watt's steam engine
1780	Thomas Robinson invents the kitchen range
1780s-90s	The Ragged Schools and Sunday Schools movements begin
1791	Death of John Wesley, the founder of Methodism
1795	Introduction of the Speenhamland System for dealing with the poor
1802	Health and Morals of Apprentices Act
1805	Battle of Trafalgar
1815	Davy safety lamp introduced for use by coal miners
1815	The Corn Law introduced
1815	Battle of Waterloo
1819	Massacre of Peterloo
1819	Birth of the future Queen Victoria
1820	George III dies, George IV becomes king
1828	London University founded
1829	Country's first professional police force formed in London
1832	Parliamentary Reform Act
1833	Factory Act

Glossary

cowpox a disease of cows which, when given to humans by vaccination, gives immunity against smallpox

crossing sweeper someone, often a poor child, who swept a path through the mud and dirt of the streets to allow better-off people to cross without spoiling their clothes. The sweeper was given a tip for this service

dame school school run by a middle-aged or elderly woman who, in return for a few pence, kept an eye on small children and taught them a little reading and writing

enclosure the enclosing, by hedging or fencing, of previously open agricultural land. Enclosed land, at first, was largely used for grazing and not as arable land

fagging a public school custom which permitted senior boys to use junior ones almost as their servants for various tasks

flying shuttle machine patented by John Kay in 1733 which enabled one man to weave cloth instead of two as before

horsedrill horse-drawn machine invented by Jethro Tull to enable seed for crops to be sown more evenly and so less wastefully

horsehoe another of Jethro Tull's inventions, this horse-drawn hoe for weeding crops speeded up the laborious task which had previously been done by hand

Methodism a form of Protestantism which grew from the revival within the Church of England led by John and Charles Wesley in the early 18th century

mudlarks children who searched the river mudbanks for things to sell. Often this was the only way they could earn a little money

primogeniture the custom by which the eldest son of a family inherits all the family's estates on the death of his father

ragged schools schools run by charities for poor children, to give them a little basic education

Shaftesbury Society charity concerned with poor children, named after Anthony Ashley Cooper, 7th earl of Shaftesbury, who worked hard to bring about reforms affecting children, especially to improve their working conditions

smallpox a severe virus disease causing fever, skin disfigurement and often death

Spinning Jenny machine for spinning many threads at once

spinning mule machine for twisting and winding wool or cotton

trappers small children who worked the trap doors in coal mines

workhouse a public institution which gave poor people food and accommodation in return for work

Places to Visit

All the following museums have good sections dealing with life in the Industrial Revolution, whether it was agricultural changes or new methods of technology.

Birmingham City Museum and Art Gallery — department of Science and Industry
Blackburn Museum and Art Gallery
Ironbridge Gorge Museum, Telford, Salop
Leeds City Museum — Abbey House Museum
Lincoln City and County Museum — Museum of Lincolnshire Life
                            — Church Farm Museum
London — Dickens House, Doughty St, WC1
        — Science Museum, Exhibition Road, SW7
        — Wellcome Museum of Medical Science, Euston Road, NW1
Manchester — Northwestern Museum of Science and Industry
Pilkington Glass Museum, St Helens, Lancashire
Sheffield City Museum — Abbeydale Industrial Hamlet
               — Shepherd Wheel grinding shop
National Museum of Wales — North Wales Quarrying Museum, Llanberis, Gwynedd

Books for Further Reading

Avery, Gillian and Bull, Angela, *Nineteenth Century Children*, Hodder and Stoughton
Brander, Michael, *The Georgian Gentleman*, Saxon House, 1973
Briggs, Asa (ed.), *How They Lived* (vol 3), Basil Blackwell, 1969
Clarke, John, *The Price of Progress*, Hart-Davis, 1977
Hart, R.W., *England Expects*, Wayland, 1972
Jarrett, Derek, *England in the Age of Hogarth*, Hart-Davis, 1974
Laver, James, *The Age of Illusion*, Weidenfeld, 1972
Quennell, M. and C.H.B., *A History of Everyday Things in England III*, Batsford, 1961
Rooke, Patrick, *The Age of Dickens*, Wayland, 1970

Index

The numbers in **bold type** refer to the figure numbers of the illustrations